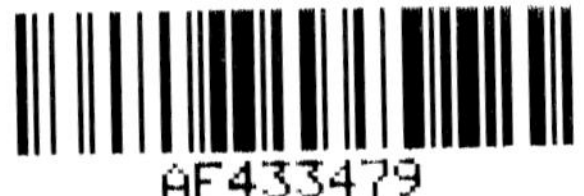

Whispers of the Nocturne

Whispers of the Nocturne

Matthew Petchinsky

Whispers of the Nocturne
By Matthew Petchinsky

| 9 | -

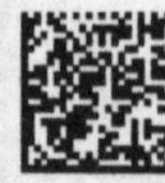

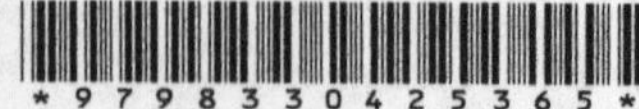